MW01119955

Copyright © 2013
All rights reserved.

ISBN 978-1-291-41089-1

For the worms:

When I'm gone, enjoy.

Poems

Prose

<u>Poems</u>

Words of Warning

Be weary of the gods

Be weary of those who make gods of other people

Be weary of other people

Be weary of yourself, though I'm sure you already are

Be weary of weariness

Be weary of teariness, which will greet you as an old friend or lover and take you on long moonlit walks at midnight into your self

Be weary of money, rich people kill themselves every day

Be weary of love, people in love kill themselves every day

Be weary of anything and everything, you will have to give it all up sooner or later

And be weary of me. I don't know what the fuck I'm talking about.

A Haiku For Every Girl I've Ever Slept With

1. The haiku form is
Of an appropriate length
To describe this fuck

2. When I handcuffed you
It was so insanely hot
I came in my jeans

3. We used to have sex
So we didn't have to talk
Now we do neither

4. We had a threesome
You, me and my depression
Depression fucks hard

5. I shouted my love
From the rooftops before
Almost jumping off

6. You didn't like me
But you did like my writing
I guess that's enough

7. Entangled, twitching
We came down as cenotaphs
Numb with limbless minds

8. Tried your fantasy
And pretended to rape you.
It felt a bit forced.

9. You learned of my pain
And said you'd try to fix me
That wasn't your job

10. You weren't attractive
But alcohol and codeine
Made a mess of me

11. You liked to be choked
You stuffed animals for fun
You were just my type.

12. Halfway through you sobbed
Said you were touched as a child
I stopped and held you

13. 13 is bad luck
But three's a lucky number
14 would agree

14. It wasn't awkward
It was just double the fun
That's arithmetic

15. Puked everywhere
And then fell into a bush
You still wanted me

16. Our contrasting skin
Meant some passersby would stare
And we just loved it

17. You were a model
Who found me through my writing
Thank you, internet

18. We made a sex tape
I hope I find it before
My family does

19. I whipped you too hard
Inadvertently drew blood
Apologised quick

20. Cars drove by as I
Fingered you at a bus stop
(A romantic date)

21. It's strange to think it
But before you miscarried
Was I a father?

22. We both got naked
Online for our followers
In different ways

23. "You don't care" you said
So I pretended to cry
And then we had sex

24. You liked taking charge
And I went along with it
Out of laziness

25. I tried to whip you
Then I hit my testicles
It ruined the mood

26. It took twenty five
Twenty five misconnections
Before I found you

Hologram

Physicists believe this dimension
may be nothing more than a hologram

But they have not run their fingertips
down the curve of your back

Why I'm Here (Still)

At 10 years old I asked my dad how much it hurt to slit your throat.

A lot, he said. It would hurt everyone who loved me.

Breaking up with Myself

Dear Myself,
It's not you, it's me
(But you are me, so it sort of is you)

Dear Myself,
I'm tired of fighting
I always come crawling back, but not this time
We're growing apart

Dear Myself, I need to find myself
Not you
A new myself
A better one
I'm shedding you like reptilian skin

Dear Myself,
I know we got kicked around
but you didn't have to take it out on me
and beat me blue
and senseless
every
fucking
night

Dear Myself,
I drown you in whiskey
I always wake up with you the next morning
I need space

Dear Myself,
I'm a different person now
I've moved on
We're done
(Apart from the occasional fling)

I wish I wrote the way I thought

I wish I wrote the way I thought
Obsessively
Incessantly
With maddening hunger
I'd write to the point of suffocation
I'd write myself into nervous breakdowns
Manuscripts spiraling out like tentacles into
abysmal nothing
And I'd write about you
a lot more
than I should

What I Have To Offer

On trains in London you are told to mind the gap
And the gap is a gap between people

They do not talk or make eye contact
The solitude is protocol
But at 1 in the morning
If an elderly piss-stinking drunkard gets on
Dribbling, jabbering gibberish
The people will laugh
And smile at each other
They are in this together now

We need the drunkards
And in later life
It is a service
I am happy
To provide

Haiku # 1
Wanting is painful
But wanting to not want things
Is problematic

Haiku # 2
Let me stay in bed
Until it envelops me
And I am mattress

Haiku # 3
Let me stay silent
Until words regain flavour
Free from awkwardness

Haiku # 4
A passerby said:
"He doesn't have anyone"
It made me quite sad

Haiku # 5 (A Suicide Note)
Looked in the freezer
There were no chicken nuggets
It was the last straw

Haiku # 6
My heart is a sun
A billion tons of heat
Please gravitate in

Electrons

Electrons can communicate instantly,
whether a meter away
or a billion miles apart
they are connected

I wish
we were
electrons

Miniature sun

I found a little speckle of warmth somewhere
I had been looking for it for a while
A coruscating orb
I clasped it to my chest
I'm not sure if it's there or not
But it feels real enough, some of the time
I keep it in my pocket
Away from everyone else
And sometimes it's light enough
To stumble home with

God

She said on the phone:
"Maybe God just forgot about you.
There's no plan in your name.
You've just been left to piss in public,
Leave your rubbish everywhere
And ignore the neighbours"

I'm a man of faith.
There couldn't be a God who'd let us mutilate
ourselves
The way we do.
I have faith in that.

But they say
The flit
Of a wing
Of a butterfly
On the other side of the planet
Is enough to change the course of human history

I have a god
After all.

I worship
The butterfly
That brought me
To you

Message in the Sand

I grabbed a twig and in the sand
My torment I transcribed

That worry washed away
As you swept in - a tender tide

The Feeling of You

The feeling of you is the feeling of
God against skin
Or to drift off
Between train stops
A symbiotic brain bop
A sizzling syzygy of sibilance
The rap-a-tap rhythm of rapture
When we nap blanket wrapped
By lava lamp

Sometimes I still miss
The feeling
Of you

An Exhibition of Myself

In science museums
children discover how small they are,
learning about the ever expanding
enormity of space
and for some reason
there are no counselors standing by

My parents watched over my shoulder
as I had my picture taken by a machine
that could digitally age your face

I looked into the eyes of my future self
wrinkled, bald, peppered with liver spots

I burst into tears,
realising I was going to die one day

In time
this would not scare me
much at all

Sound

Sometimes
all I want is
                silence
but the body
is a sack of sound
air rasps, hisses and wheezes
down a cacophonous esophagus
in and out of lungs
as though we were flutes

the heart beats
the blood pumps
the joints creak

perhaps we are grooves
on a record stretching light years across
playing in another dimension
where extraterrestrial angels shake their hips
and flirt and fuck and fall in love
to the rhythm of our endurance

even if there is no one listening
I like to dream
of that miracle melody

Deaf and Dumb and Blind

I thought if I was deaf and dumb and blind
I might reside in darkness pain forgot
But still I'd know the torture in my mind
Of what it is to touch you, and to not

Mr and Mrs

Mr and Mrs
sit down to a dinner made of
blood, sweat and body tissue
by candlelight

Mr tightens his impromptu tourniquet
The blood stains the carpet

"You are what you eat" he jokes
He is junk food

She takes a mouthful of him
Biting off more than she can chew
He is hard to swallow

They eat their hearts out

They consume
but never
consummate

They will feast
and feast
and feast away

at themselves and each other

until they are no more
than wisps of nothing

The Music-makers

When you listen to music more beautiful
than anything
you'll ever be able
to offer the world

And it hurts

Take solace in the fact that
you and the music-makers
once inhabited the same
golf ball of energy,
before it stretched out
into light years
of everything

Childhood Haikus

1. Strawberry ice cream
And robots and dinosaurs
And Crash Bandicoot

2. I had a stutter
So I avoided speaking
No big d-d-deal

3. I painted pictures
Old curtains made a cool cape
And I loved the swings

4. I would always cry
After the social workers
Sent Daddy away

5. Brainwashed by TV
I would throw up in the sink
To not be chubby

6. I was only five
But I'd climb up jungle gyms
And threaten to jump

7. The names I got called
Still echo around my head
And sometimes deafen

Tonight

The unknowingly gifted misfits
With dimmed wits and slit wrists
Sniff dizz and hit piff to get lifted. They sit stiff
In their bedrooms
By their computers
Dreaming of fucking each other
And they will
But not
Tonight

Tonight they have only themselves

The loneliness takes root like a weed and rots them
from the inside
They rot and peel and melt and flake
They watch The Only Way Is Essex
and get faded because they want to fade away

But the misfits have a mistress:
Each night
Sleep saves
And submerges them
In the glistening waters
Of their own minds

Words scribbled onto a receipt on the tube

I am tranquillised and tranquil
as this train trembles and clanks through
all the dim synaptic tunnels ever
buzzing in my brain
and I breathe and rest my head back
and forget regrets and setbacks
as if bleeding all my darkness
down an interstellar drain

Bullet Points

- If I skin my heart with a potato peeler how
  many layers til nothing?

- I bought a scratch card
  but when I scratched it off
  it said I had food and clean water
  and should be fucking grateful as it is

- Many primates express themselves
  by hurtling fecal matter
  (which explains these poems)

The End of Everything

in the playground
children tormented each other
and then grew up to rape, and kill,
or both, in either order

but this was not enough

we set the earth aflame
in a spectacular nuclear holocaust
billions died screaming
skin bubbled furiously and melted away
people peeled
and as if that wasn't enough
I was on my period

not many made it into the shelters in time
now I cannot remember
the feeling of sun against my skin
or skin against my skin

my bunker is closed in and dark
but I feel no less confined
than I did by train carriages at rush hour,
my small office cubicle
or my lonely flat

Holy Wine and Honky-Tonk

Science, you can have my organs
I don't want them

Make me a coat rack
Fuck me with a vacuum
Dissect me on live television
On all the kids' channels

Or let me live inside a honky-tonk piano
and feed me holy wine through a tube

The family argues
If the TV stays off longer than ten minutes
And every second brings me closer to
~~my destiny~~ another empty second

School for Boys

I remember the kid who got choke slammed
To the dinner hall floor
(He was lifted out by an ambulance helicopter)

And the kids who trained their dogs
To fight for sport

And the kid who got mauled by those dogs
Outside the playground

And the kids who got mugged and bullied
And had to learn to be two inches tall

And the kids who wore gang colours
And got knifed to death
For living in the wrong post code

And the grown-ups who told us
These were the happiest
Days of our lives

Safe Word

Our safe word was buttons

I'm not sure why you chose it

Perhaps it was the way those b's and t's
hit like my belt to your bottom
or the way it sizzled out with a '*sssss*'…

But I'm glad you had a word

I've whispered a thousand words
to the heavens

and none of them
saved me
from myself

Mara's Daughters

Enough of the others, who are no more than
bacteria in sweatshop chic

Enough of being gang banged
by Mara's daughters

Enough howling into hollow chests

Enough of the magazines
that tell you you're worthless,
put them in a box
with your unanswered prayers

This life is a blood sport
But you are miraculous

An angel
worthy of the stars
that birthed you

To feel so intensely is a gift
And the hunger you feel
Is a malnourished love

Feed it

<u>Prose</u>

The Empty

The longer I live, the further I am thrust into my conviction that beauty lies in the empty. As hard as we may try to feel complete, that emptiness is ever there, staring us in the face. The persistence of this void, its undeniable stubbornness, goes some way to persuade me that God willed it to be there - because he saw it to be beautiful. Nothingness is silence, peace and promise, and because atoms are predominantly made of vacuum, we too are predominantly empty. Perhaps God was intent on making nothing, and had to make do with us, the weed that grew between.

Synesthesia

We all have five senses. For Lina, they had always
overlapped. She could touch sounds, hear sights.
She knew the taste of echoing piano chords, she
had been physically caressed by string sections.

She could not communicate to anyone how
overwhelming everything felt, how tender and
sensitive she was to the raw beauty her world
radiated. A walk through the park was an assault to
the senses, a bombardment. She could smell the
sun beaming, touch the bird song.

As well as five senses, Lina had five boyfriends.
But as her senses blurred, so did they. The way she
felt when one boyfriend touched her conjured up
the face of another, the way one boyfriend tasted
would be another's voice. Soon they all merged,
and she could not tell what began where. It did not
matter. The whos and whats melted into a single
pure love. She realised they were not people at all.
They were sounds. Drums, strings, song. She could
be alone as long as she had music because inside
each song for her were a million lovers and a
million parks.

Words Written Drunk at 4 AM

I want quite desperately to be a person, but I'm not. I'm a billion different conflicting characters, trying to inhabit a gelatinous slab. Sometimes I imagine them. A billion different versions of myself, marching towards me across a grassy knoll. I snipe them down from my clock tower. Bam. Bam. Bam. I blanket the green in exquisite red; brains split, splice, splat, splash, splosh, splatter and sputter, and I flutter as I slaughter my contradictions, leaving only one survivor. Finally, I am coherent. I know who I am. I'm that guy. That guy on the grass, and no one can take that away from me. But then, sometimes, and I don't know why, I pull the trigger on him too.

The Hum

It began as a low hum. I couldn't work out where it was coming from, but it wouldn't stop. This incessant grinding groan that whirred and whirred and unfurled everything in me into a long nervous tendril ready to snap at any moment. The hum was becoming louder and louder. The hum was becoming a scream.

Few people were allowed in because everything was always a mess. But when they were, they couldn't hear it. If I tried to describe it to them they acted as though I was humming to myself. As though I should pull myself together. There were a couple of kind words, but they got harder and harder to hear over the hum. After a while I stopped letting people in at all.

The medication wasn't working. I was having trouble eating and sleeping. The house just screamed and screamed into my head all day. It became harder and harder to leave. The door hinges seemed stiff, the handle heavy. After a while I could not leave at all, something was holding me in. I just lay in bed all day. Sprawled out and crucified, my temples throbbing from the shrill drilling howl kicking me in the skull. It grew louder and louder, but I think it was always there. Ringing in my ears. I remember the childhood that taught me to fear people. I remember: ten years old, the hum told me to slit my throat.

I am locked in now. The window is my only porthole out of the pain. I watch the world from behind a sheet of glass. The sunrises are flickering pools of purple light, and the sunsets are red as blood. They're beautiful, but veiled by a crowd of trees, and at night the clouds shroud the stars. Blurry figures appear at my window, concerned faces, silhouettes of people I once felt close to. Their voices muffle. I feel no warmth for them now. All I feel is the bellowing shriek. I've started drinking. It's less loud when I drink.

I have to kill it. I throw a brick through the window. Topple the wardrobe. Sweep everything to the floor. The screaming soars. I can't stop the hum. I am the hum. I take a sledgehammer to the wall, pounding holes into its blank indifference. Nothing's enough. I need the ceiling to cave in on me. I set the desk aflame and wait. The fire spreads like an outstretched heart, its static calls out to me as the house wails and moans and roars in pain. The monster collapses in on itself. Slowly the scream subsides and I slip into sleep. I am swallowed up by endless white, and the ethereal relief of pure orgasmic nothing.

Dreams of Autotomy

I wandered wherever my dog-tired eyes would take
me; round mountainous tower blocks, down dirty
roads with sexed up billboards, past herds of
masked commuters marching soundless down the
pavement. Down about down payments. Terrified
of eye contact. Terrified of being poor. Terrified of
anything other than bed. Battered and dazed and
dozy and dopey and dosed up on caffeine and
ignorance, fiending for something that was under
their noses, but using those noses only to snort up
Charlie, or to press against computer screens.
Wanting, always wanting. And I was one of them.
Heart in my mouth, I stumbled into an alleyway
and proceeded to heave, wiping away the
remaining dribble of spew with my cuff, before
going back to meet the boys for a smoke and a fix
of McDonalds mush.

I dragged myself onto the tube and curled up in the
corner, staring down at the crowd's feet. Sandals,
leather, Supras. Drenched in the scent of it all.
Hurtling through tunnels. All of us a disgusting
waterfall of energy and bubbling flesh, crashing
round the carriage, clinging to anything it could. I
turned away. Sat and closed my eyes and hummed
to myself. Slipped the penknife out of my pocket,
the one Uncle Trevor had given me for my 16th
birthday. Flicked open the various options of knife,
scissor and corkscrew before making my decision,
or incision, and placed my left hand down firm on
the dusty tube floor, contemplating which finger to

pick first. It seemed logical to go with the thumb and then work anti-clockwise round the hand. No one looked up from their newspapers or Kindles. I began to slice into the thumb. It was tougher than I had anticipated, and I had to use a sawing motion to tear through the muscle. Halfway through I began to consider what I'd order when I got to McDonalds. McNuggets, I decided. No. A burger with McNuggets inside. Then I got to my stop and got off, leaving my thumb in the puddle where it was.

The buildings were covered in graffiti, tagged up by the drones from my school wanting to leave a mark on the colony. I left my mark by pissing behind a bush and then greeted the guys, all velvet eyes and stupid grins, rolling up a jay. I make a couple jokes that no one laughs at and secretly chastise myself for it. Curtis doesn't notice I'm passing him the zoot with a thumbless hand. I wonder if he might have similar invisible wounds. He seems happy. That's the problem. There's no real way of knowing who people really are, who they are on the inside. Your thoughts are yours and yours alone. It's so lonely to think. Having to hear yourself talk all day. I wished we could think collectively. Do away with the compromised mumbo jumbo of language, just share our thoughts, unfiltered and true. Instead I'm stuck in my head, wondering what it's like in theirs. We communicate only in stoned drawl: "Fam, fam, I love you bares you know", and more importantly; "Man's kinda feeling for some chicken nuggets."

Red-eyed and empty stomached we stagger into McDonalds. It is eerily clean and white, though stained by a trail of crimson blood drops that only I can see. We wait patiently in line when I tell Curtis I need the toilet. I can feel it coming on again. I hold the sink and look into the mirror. God, I'm ugly. Hawk nose. Flaky skin. Greasy hair that tentacles out in the wrong directions. I collapse in a heap in the stall and begin sawing away once more, this time beginning near the shoulder blade. Needless to say the whole arm hurt more than the thumb, but the high helped. When I finish the blood pours out in spools like big red fingers looking, looking, looking across the porcelain floor. I left the bathroom and went to sit down with the guys, who had ordered my food for me. I tried to stay quiet as I ate my because I didn't want them to notice I was missing an arm.

I was pretty sure my friends only ever hung out with me out of pity so I rushed home. Bunged up and tired. When I get there the whole family's in the living room. None of them are talking. They're all on their laptops. The house feels dirty and cluttered. The keyboards clatter. Dad looks down. None of the meds he takes for his depression really work. Him and mum fight a lot. He likes birds. Everyone stares into their separate little screens. I get a snack from the fridge. Go upstairs. Lie down. Cocoon myself in my duvet. Put some music on. Try to get a hold of myself. Get a hold of my leg. Cut. Cut. Cut. Cut. Cut. And there. That spectacular explosion of red ribbon weaving its way across the white mattress, and then the drip drip drip off the edge of the bed. I chucked the leg to the side of the room. The wound kept spurting. I didn't know what to do with myself. I send Emily a text, as sending a text is easier than talking over the phone. She says she'll be over in ten minutes. I twiddle my thumbs. Well, thumb.

There's a knock on the door, I open it. There she is. Emily. I offer her something to drink, and she politely declines. We go up to my room. I try to veil my flaws but she unknowingly magnifies and mollifies them in turn. Anxieties arising and dissipating like the coming and going of the sweeping tide, or the rising and falling of our chests as we embrace, and breathe together, curled up, foetal, as though we have returned to the womb (to spoon). And we kiss as a solace from talking. And we talk as a solace from thinking. And we laugh. And laugh. And laugh. I feel lucky. She runs her fingertips up and down my body, down my chest and skinny torso, up the inside of my thigh, the thigh that I still have. I worry I might be breathing too loud. Or too fast. I worry I won't get hard. Or I will get hard, and I'll come. I worry that she won't like the way I'm touching her. That it won't look like it does on television. That it'll be awkward and self-conscious and uncomfortable. I worry she'll be able to tell how much I'm worrying. I worry that she'll notice my missing limbs. In all my worrying I get too caught up in my head, and by the time I look down, I realise I'm already sawing away at my other leg. I try to go through with things anyway, spreading her legs and entering her, mutilating myself the entire time. I thrust myself and the saw back and forth, back and forth. Tearing through flesh. Through bone. The pain becomes too much and I collapse, embarrassed, making apologies to her, sawing away ever faster until I rip through the final bit of skin. I hold her. The blood showers out like a fountain. I lie there exploding and consider whether to next go for the head.

Moths

I've read that the reason moths appear to be attracted to light is because they use the moon to navigate. When they encounter an electric light they try to treat it the same as the moon, and end up battering themselves about the light bulb in confusion. This is our struggle. If there is a God, or any eternal truth, we're just disorientated by an earthly imitation of it.

Under Your Skin

You get out of bed. Your body doesn't. This is, understandably, somewhat disconcerting. You have often used the phrase 'over my dead body', but logic dictated you the least likely person to ever be in that position. If only the universe were governed by logic. Instead, here you are, staring down at yourself. What you had once considered intrinsic to your very being is now an empty shell. How peaceful your old form seems now, free of woe and worried thought. Its absence of consciousness seems akin to tranquility. Perhaps your body is better off without you.

Not having a mirror to hand, or a hand, you float to the bathroom to get a look at yourself. You look in the mirror and there is no one there to hate any more. You are a cloud of energy, a miniature nebula. You leave the house, and everyone else is the same. A floating fog of nothingness. A haze.

No one knows what to do. No haircuts, no make up, no work outs, no food, no clothes, no booze, no drugs. No sex. Everyone looks the same. There is nothing to buy. Nothing to work for. A consumerist culture crumbled over night.

You go on your first *truly* blind date. You don't know how old they are or whether they're a man or woman. It doesn't really matter. You feel as though you've made a connection. You've finally made a connection and you're not alone. Or empty. Or

bored with life. They are not out of your league.
There is no league.

We come to realise we are not islands onto
ourselves. Separation is an illusion and everything
is intertwined. We become a single consciousness.
A mass cloud of interconnected energy. Which is
sad really, because though few of us realised it,
that's all we ever were.

Exit Chip

"I hope the exit is joyful and hope never to return"
- Frida Kahlo's last words

I had a dream my family were driving me through Switzerland, to a suicide clinic. Gut-stomping ugliness shot passed the window, but it was beautiful because I was looking at it for the last time. Moment by moment I let go of the whole idea of having moments. I felt nauseous looking at the little languid people pacing the pavements, plaguing the planet like a cancer. Content in their mediocrity. The pavements repulsed me. Give people the chance to pave the world over in any colour, and of course, they choose grey. The car was a warm womb though, and my family were happy to drive me to my death because they knew it was what I wanted. When I got out of the car, they just smiled and waved, as if to say "See you on the other side." There was no other side, but that was how I liked it. Everything made sense.

Waking up felt how a raindrop must feel, hurtling into a window and then slowly drizzling down it. I'd be drizzling out all day. I got out of bed and lurched for my whiskey. I had started drinking again. Smoking too. I'm not sure why. Perhaps I had begun to fetishise my own self-destruction. I went outside without bothering to put shoes on, and the ground felt cold and damp against my bare skin. I crouched down and had a smoke with a snail. The snail didn't say much, and

I liked that about him. He just felt his way around. I tried to stare into space but there was all this other stuff in the way. I thought about Dad. It had been a month since he died. Well, he didn't really die. Not recently anyway. It's complicated. I ran over in my head what the doctor had told me.

"So... In most cases I'd be professionally obligated not to tell you this, but in this instance, a potential legal loophole should probably be brought to your attention now, to avoid any awkwardness later." He scratched his bulbous nose with thick heavy fingers and adjusted his glasses. He looked dirty, which felt odd - doctors were supposed to be clean. The room was white and sterile though. Clinical and cold, it matched his indifference, if not his hygiene.

"A loophole?"

"Yes, a loophole. Essentially, your father as you once knew him has not just died. Only his body has. Your father has, for the last..." he glanced down his chart, "...twenty years, been operated by a small computer chip in his brain. We call it an 'Exit Chip'."

"I don't - What?"

"Your father was one of the first to have them installed. Imagine you're crippled by clinical depression, and you want to die. The only thing holding you back is the guilt of leaving your friends and family behind, leaving them behind and hurting them."

I didn't have to imagine.

"What this chip does is copy the basic biological functions of the human brain, allowing the person to be essentially brain dead, while the computer chip runs the body on autopilot. Essentially allowing you to die, but still walk and talk for the benefit of your loved ones. Patterns of thought, memories, moral values remain. But in reality you are a complete zombie. I could have one and you wouldn't be able to tell the difference."

It seemed too elaborate to be a joke. Besides, I wasn't sure this man was capable of humour. "So my relationship with my father for the last twenty years has been a lie?"

"I'm not saying that, Mr. Elliot. You could have had many meaningful experiences with your father, he just wasn't alive for them."

I stared at him blankly.

"Now... Normally I would not be telling you this, because it rather defeats the purpose of having the implant if your family ultimately finds out anyway. But in this case it transpires that, because your father was one of the first to have this device installed, the proper administration had not yet been put into place, and certain documents that should have been signed, were not. Your father wrote a will shortly before his body died, but because for all intents and purposes it was not actually him, this could be challenged in a court of law. That's the legal loophole I was referring to earlier. Do you understand?"

I nodded. A swirl of questions surged my head, but somehow the first one to travel down the synapses and out of my mouth was:

"How much would it take to have it done?"

Not as much as I thought, it turned out. I had it installed late last night, before bed. It takes 24 hours for the chip to gradually become fully functioning, and the doctor warned me I would feel my mind slipping away from me as the day went on. It was only the morning and I couldn't feel it yet. I was pretty sure I still had most of me in there. I just felt less afraid than usual. No longer the zoned and moaning acrimonious drone. Sleep awaited me. Those were Henry Ford's last words; "I'll sleep well tonight". I wondered what my last words would be. Probably something about fucking. Fucking was the one thing I'd miss. Intimacy with other human beings was one of the nicer things, but certainly not worth living a life over. I had no desire to get a job or make money. Go out on the weekends. Start a family. Retire.

None of it interested me. I had grown tired of dependency. Dependency on medication and alcohol and drugs and people. Tired of being a burden. I was really just ready to go. I'd tried life on for size and found it tight and uncomfortable. It was itchy and rode up on the brain.

I read about a monk named Godhika who killed himself. The Buddha said through suicide he had liberated himself from all desire, even the desire to live, and had thus achieved enlightenment. "Such indeed is how the steadfast act: They are not attached to life. Having drawn out craving at its root, Godhika has attained final Nirvana". That's what awaited me – final Nirvana. I began to think of myself as the ultimate escape artist.

I called up Mum. I just wanted to hear her voice one last time. She told me about the dog and how well-behaved it was during their walk. She told me how things were at the office, and about how much she missed Dad. I didn't have the heart to tell her about the chip. His or mine. In the end the legal issues were settled according to standard Exit Chip company policy, and everyone agreed it was for the best that she didn't find out. We talked about my sisters, who were doing well in school, and about the awful weather. She said she had to go. Her blueberry muffins were done. I told her to send my love to the whole family. She said she would, and that she loved me too. "Things are hard right now", she said, "but they'll get better. I promise." I wished I could believe her. Then I choked up a little, trying to say 'goodbye' as casually as possible. She said 'see you soon'. After I hung up I couldn't move for a long time. It's better this way, I told myself. This way you won't be a burden.

I still took my pill today, which didn't make much sense when I thought about it, given the circumstances. I was glad I wasn't on the old stuff because it used to give me panic attacks, and I was glad I wasn't still secretly doubling it, because that was making them doubly worse. I needed more cigarettes and for a moment couldn't remember where the shop was. My mind's already leaving me, I thought.

The shopkeeper gave me my change and said "See you tomorrow." He would see me, but I wouldn't see him. I went outside and lit up. There was a beautiful woman a few yards away, leggy with a short brown bob, pouty red lips. The kind of woman you only see in 50s pin-up calendars or vintage porn. Her dress was loose but I could tell she had a great arse. I had a sudden and very real urge to fuck her. I only had a day so I couldn't do what I'd usually do - fall in love with her and then fall out of love with her and then fall in love with the memory of being in love with her. But I would've done all that ad infinitum for that arse. She broke me out of my brain babbling, asking for a lighter. I handed it over.

"Nice weather we're having" I said. This was sarcastic, because it wasn't nice. It had been raining. It wasn't a particularly witty thing to say. I'm an idiot, I thought. She chuckled under her breath. I tried again.

"What do you want your last words to be?" I asked. That's much worse, I thought. Now it sounds like I'm going to murder her.

"What?" She looked puzzled. I wasn't sure if she had heard me or not. The 'What?' would be warranted in either case. Her already pouty lips now pouted in a quizzical manner, her brow furrowed.

"Just, I was reading some. Last words, I mean. Churchill's were 'I'm so bored with it all'. And Austen's were 'I want nothing but death'... Cheerful stuff."

"I don't really think it matters what your last words are. They're all important. Every single stupid word, shooting all the way back to birth. Every single fucking poorly thought out word"

I just nodded and said "That's a lot of pressure. Now the next thing you say has to be important"

She looked at me with big pools of water for eyes and thought for a second, before asking:

"Do you want to go for a walk?"

I hesitated. I had intended to spend my last day shuffling around the house listening to Schubert or Smetana, taking long baths and feeling sorry for myself. Maybe even trying to write a short story before I went. Do something other than consume. Human interaction was always a gamble, but today was my last hand. I wasn't sure I could say no to those legs though. Those thigh high socks.

"Sure." I asked her her name, and she said it was Mae. "Like the month, but, with an 'e'." She had scars on her wrists which I thought made her all the more beautiful and I wasn't sure why. I held her hand. I wasn't afraid because I knew I didn't have much time. Any newly arising anxieties wouldn't live through the night. We walked past pretty flowers and drugged up old people mumbling gobbledegook to themselves, which was probably better than keeping the gobbledegook cooped. Walking around felt weird, like strolling through a dysfunctional ant colony. A funeral procession paraded past. She said she thought the flowers on the hearse were really pretty, and wondered how something so beautiful could have a dead person inside. I told her she was really beautiful. I think she thought it was a similar thing.

We talked and talked and talked. I asked her if she believed in love, and she smiled and said it was her most elaborate method of self-harm. As the day went on I began to like her more and more. We walked by a pond with a lone swan, the sun had come out and the way the light glimmered and glittered on the surface of the water was really breath-taking. The orange trees shed their crumpled leaves. I felt as though I was one of those trees, this chip was shedding my crumpled self. Then I remembered it was Spring, and I didn't understand why the trees would be orange in Spring. Perhaps my brain had shut down more than I realised. I wasn't perceiving the trees any more, my subconscious was filling in the gaps. What if I was hallucinating the entire park?

I started to wonder if Mae was even real. She must be real, I thought, I could feel her holding my hand. Her hands were soft and warm and electric. No, she must be real - my swampy brain couldn't conjure up anyone so angelic. What if it could? I wasn't sure it mattered. All people are hallucinations, anyway. You can never really know all of someone. Their souls are locked away somewhere in their head, and you'll never be able to get in there. The best you can do is fall in love with the idea of someone. Falling in love with the idea of her was okay with me. Or the idea of the idea of her. It was the first time in a long time I'd fallen in love with the idea of anything other than escape.

It felt like it might be a good idea to tell her I was dying, but I figured it was a bit of a downer.

If we met up tomorrow she wouldn't be able to tell the difference anyway. There was a woman jiggling and jogging in sweats with a big stomach that bounced with every pace. She was probably jogging to get rid of that stomach. I felt bad for her. Maybe she was jogging to look like the photo-shopped girls.

"If you could be reincarnated as any animal," I asked, "which animal do you think you would pick?"

"Probably a house cat. Just an average run of the mill kind of tabby cat. With kindly bohemian owners and no children. Actually yeah, my owners can be an infertile couple that redirect their parental urges towards me."

"Wouldn't you rather be a more-than-average cat? Like an extraordinary cat. With telepathic powers or something."

"I'd rather have the simple life of a mediocre feline. Unless I could be a cat that did people things, that would be cool."

"What people things would you want to do? Like, if you're gonna do people things you might as well just be a person" I reasoned.

"Things that would freak people out. I'd prey on people. Wait for a person to be looking at me on the window sill with nobody else watching, and then start reading a newspaper or write in a diary or play dice."

I laughed. "They'll think they're mentally ill, that's cruel. Why would you want to fuck with people?"

"Just for fun" she said, smirking.

I wondered what she could possibly like about me. With my pained, angular yet somehow drooping face, like a wounded bird, and my dirty bushy hair and piercing serpent laugh of nervousness, awkward and disappointed in my own company. She was beautiful. She had the kind of face that could make you want to shout from the rooftops, rather than jump off.

"So, um, you seeing anyone?" I asked.

"A couple guys. I don't know, my therapist says I 'collect relationships to make up for an adolescence characterised by rejection'."

"Yeah, I think I do that too. But I'm starting to realise that no matter how many people you fuck it won't make up for the shit you went through as a kid."

"Fun to try though."

I rubbed her hand gently with the tip of my thumb. "Yeah, it's fun to try."

We got out of the other side of the park. I couldn't remember the name of the park. I actually couldn't remember my name. I liked that feeling. I looked at my watch. I guess it was getting a little later on in the day. I could see my flat. An average flat I was able to rent with my average income from my average performance at my average job.

"That's my flat," I told her.

"Oh. Well, this is probably the bit where you invite me in for a glass of wine."

"Oh… I don't have any wine."

"Any beverage would work really".

"I ask right now?"

"Right now would work, I mean… If not now, when, y'know?" She had more of a point than she realised. I felt a lump in my throat and sweat on my palms and my heartbeat was fast and it was very hard to act smooth with all that going on. My door was blue and that seemed like it could be correct but I really couldn't get a picture of it in my mind.

"Well, I was totally going to ask any way… So now you've ruined the spontaneity of it."

"Oh, okay. I'll pretend like I didn't say anything." We waited for a moment. I looked at my shoes. They were kind of blurry. "Do you want to come in?"

"Wow, that totally caught me off guard. But since you're asking, sure."

I fumbled about in my pocket for my keys. I wondered if she could tell that I had only been working with half a brain this whole time (already being a half-wit that had me down to about a quarter). We walked up the stairs for what seemed like a long time and didn't say anything or make eye contact. I gently rubbed her side, right above her waist. She didn't seem to mind but she was quiet. When we got in I had to sit down because I was feeling a little dizzy. I tried to wriggle my toes and then realised I couldn't feel them any more. The chip must be controlling them now. I wanted to touch her before I lost feeling in my hands. Her legs were crossed towards me, and her thighs looked thick and smooth. I went to touch them, but then she turned her head to me, and I quickly retreated.

"I like your place" she said. I didn't.

"Oh, thanks. Me too."

"So, you mentioned your dad had a heart attack before. I'm really sorry, that must be really hard."

"What?" I tried to process the words in my head but I couldn't really work them out. My Dad had a heart attack. I thought about it. I couldn't really picture him, which frightened me. I must have had a father at some point, I thought. People usually do.

"I don't, um… I can't… I can't really remember him". I realised what was happening. I couldn't remember my mother either. They were blurs to me. I remembered their warmth but not their faces, where they lived or what had happened to them. "He had a heart attack?"

"That's what you told me."

"Oh."

"You forgot that?"

"Yeah. Yeah I guess so. No, you're right. I mean, that sounds right."

This is probably when I should tell her, I thought.

"That's okay," she said. "I've… I've been

forgetting stuff all day. For a second I wasn't sure why I was here. I couldn't tell you my phone number."

"I think mine has some 7's in it"

"...Do you have a chip too, Edward?"

I couldn't believe it. She knew it was her last day on earth and she spent it going for a walk with me. Suddenly I didn't feel like dying so much any more. But I would, and so would she. I looked into her eyes and they looked a little sad. I nodded. She rubbed my arm a little.

"I hope that... when we're not ourselves any more... I hope that we keep this going."

"Me too." I moved a little closer to her.

"We don't have very long left." she said.

"I know". She looked down. I took a deep breath and put my arm around her waist. I leaned in, and our lips met. Softly at first. Then not so softly. I ran my hands down her torso. She ran hers through my hair. I clasped her hands and pinned her down to the floor. I fucked her hard. It felt good to switch off. Be an animal for a little while. The French call the orgasm "la petite mort", or "Little Death", and that's how it felt when we came - like we died together. A rehearsal for the ever-impending real thing.

After that we just lay there, holding each other, ready for it all to end.

"We never did work out what our last words would be," I said.

She was silent for a long moment, and then said: "I'm glad I met you."

"I wouldn't want to die with anyone else." I kissed her neck. "Maybe we'll reincarnate as telepathic cats or cats that do people things"

"I'd really rather just be nothing." "Mm, me too". She lay her head on my chest. My leg was clasped safe and tight between hers. I liked the feeling of her skin against mine. It seemed too convenient that she had a chip too. That I just met her so out of the blue. Maybe I really did dream her up. Maybe it didn't matter at all.

I remember reading somewhere that everything in the universe had a gravitational pull on everything else in the universe. I had a gravitational pull on Mae, and the fridge, and a dying sun millions of light years away. And they all had a pull on me. All of us pushing and pulling and to-ing and fro-ing and clinging and clawing away at each other, desperately and selfishly and feverishly forever as tiny ignorant rabid and raving parasitic fetuses of insanity. I felt like a tiny cog in an incomprehensibly expansive and nonsensical clock. And God is manifest in creation, so I was a part of God. But soon I'd be gone, and then I wouldn't be a part of God any more. At first the idea of being absent from the universe bothered me, but then it didn't. Absence makes the heart grow fonder, and that's why people are so fond of God.

A gaping blanket of nothing began to envelope and embrace me as I slipped silently into dreamless sleep. The room became a kaleidoscope. I wasn't sure who I was or who was next to me. I could touch them but not feel them. I tried to think about how I got here. I must have been born. Yes. Born. To a mother and father who loved me. They probably loved me. There were colours and muffled sounds and there was the sensation of air entering and exiting my lungs. I was breathing. I was breathing in and out. In. Out. In. Out. I wasn't sure where the pitch day down tell. It was starting to take a lot of energy to slick everything. I couldn't sober tree cape. Or cat. Grip. Go. Go.